Rare

Aarna Joshi

AF519327

BlueRose Publishers

First Published in December 2020

ISBN: 978-93-5427-160-1

BLUEROSE PUBLISHERS

www.bluerosepublishers.com

info@bluerosepublishers.com

+91 8882 898 898

Cover Design:

Mohd. Arif

Typographic Design:

Namrata Saini

Distributed by: BlueRose, Amazon, Flipkart, Shopclues

Note to Readers

Open your heart, Then read this book.

Dedicated

To
The Extraordinary you

Preface

In my book I discuss both my thoughts and how they changed me into a better and more mature person.

I don't know when poetry evolved from stress busting to passion for me,

And I began to write on daily basis to stay connected with my inner self,

It was like an escape for me from this hectic world.

As an avid reader, I got to know how authors beautifully expressed what they felt and that was exactly what I wanted to do,

This was a calling for me,

After sharing my experiences with others, I realized I could help them through my poems by conveying various messages.

I believe that even if this book makes even a single person feel empowered, motivated or happy and expressive then its purpose has been fulfilled.

This book is for everyone who is struggling to find their place in the world.

I hope it eases your heart.

Contents

Shilpi

Rare

"She was like a shooting star..... Rare"

Sky

She was born under the rosy sky,
raised among the wolves,
breathed the stardust,
and dissolved in the soil.

SHILPI

Knight in Shining Armour

When young she used to dream,
About her knight in shining armor,
she said he smelt like peaches and cream,
Yes, that's what she used to dream,
His hair so silky,
And skin ever so milky,
Eyes big and round,
They had many secrets bound,
His heart was so caring,
Yet on the outside he was so daring,
He rode on horses,
Travelled on roads,
swam in seas,
To fulfill any needs,
she was waiting to be rescued,
she was waiting to have drinks with him and dine,
Once a woman,
When she grew,
When she had thoughts,
And was sought,
And had loved lots,
She finally knew,
That there was no Charmer,
That she was her own,
Her own knight in shining armour.
-True

Shilpi

Shooting Star

They told her be like a shooting a star,
That others wish upon.....

A Right to Her Rights

He blessed her with talent,
But no confidence,
Thus, was kept silent.

All were impossible to convince,
any protest dealt with tough consequence.

Give a right to her rights I plead,
No command it shall be.
She is not inferior,
Nor are we superior,
So, give a right to her rights we command,
Yes, give a right to her rights we demand.

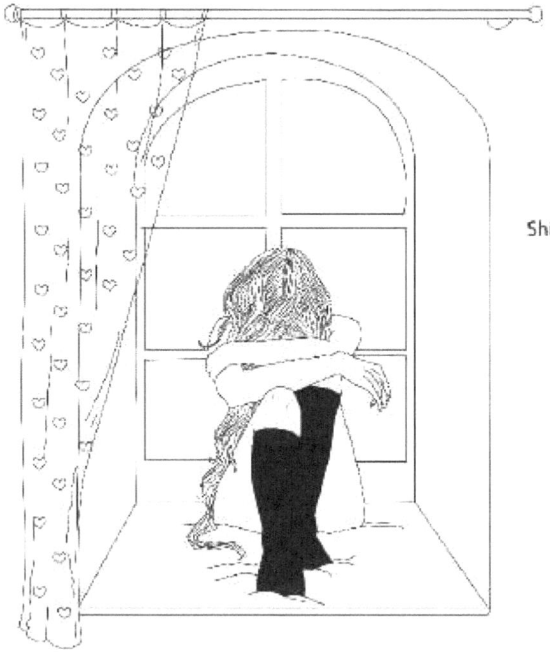

Shilpi

Destroyed

She was destroyed,
The world kept going.

-that's how it works

Deceive

A girl whose eyes were glittery,
Was shrouded in mystery,
She was such an artist,
Hid her emotions as none were to harvest,
On a face so teary,
She could fake a smile,
And radiate the scent of happiness like,
a happy chamomile,
No one knew what she thought,
Whether or not was she distraught?
Ah! How she deceived the world!
All fools and all learned,
A thousand fears,
And a million tears,
All hidden behind a beautiful smile ,
And blushing cheeks,
And happy squeaks,
There was a
girl whose eyes were glittery,
Who was shrouded in mystery..
-the mask she wears.

Shilpi

Rose

She was like a rose.....pricked when I touched her wrong
-regret oozed out.

Words

Words can be confusing,
The can be either trusting or cynical,
There are a million ways to say a word,
Words only make the world,
You Can empower one,
or Crush their spirit with just one word,
You shoot bullets from your mouth,
And hurt,
Or apply a soothing salve on someone's injured soul,
As words make the world,
Choose your words,
Well and wise,
So you don't hear desolate cries.

Fine

I am fine she said.....broken

Tears

Tears are anything but saltwater,
Releasing them will make you feel better,
Nor are they weights who make you feel heavy or,
Weigh you down or cause a simple frown,
They say tears are for the weak,
Embracing them makes you unique,
On days when you feel,
The world has ended,
When even the weather seems offended,
Let the tears flow through,
Slowly,
as the minutes tick by,
With you rocking gently,
Feeling comfort and emptiness,
That emptiness will heal you,
so let the tears flow,
Real slow,
Some tears are of happiness or pride,
When the person you see walking down the aisle is your beautiful bride,
Happy tears are a must as they,
Clear your head,
And clean your eyes,

Apply a blush of pink,
On your flushed cheeks,
That Soon you'll release happy squeaks,
And color your lips.
In bold red ink.
Tears are not admitting your fears,
They are miraculous healers,
Embrace your tears,
And have feelings to share,
And morph into a real man who cares.
-Empty

SHILPI

Distance

She felt a thousand miles away from him, though
he was just beside her.

SHILPI

Crowd

When standing amidst a crowd,
You still feel lonely....
- Soul mate

SHILPI

Receive

I am open to receive love, but no one showers any.

SHILPI

Dive

Take a deep dive into the ocean of bliss,
Whenever worried,
Feel the cool translucent waters gently touching your skin,
Feel the waves tickle you until you laugh.

Her gifts to him

She breathed fire into him,
She whispered knowledge to him,
She put care in his touch,
She gave him experience,
Yet she was betrayed.
-precious

Melt

Don't let your heart ever be like wax,
That melts at the weakest fire.

Fire

He was like fire to me.....
Bright enough offer light,
Still burned me when I got too close.

- That's why they call them crushes.

Carefree

When the world seems unfair,
When you just don't care,
When love is mere,
That is the time,
Glorious time,
When you morph from geek to chic,
looks right on fleek,
When moms just don't understand,
When you like nothing if not a brand,
Yes, Its Teenage,
the best or worst one could ever have,
When acne don't seem to stop,
Why is our hairstyle always a flop?
They say its a mere phase,
when your behavior is not at ease,
I disagree,
Its the time when you are free,
free from the duties of the world,
When you don't walk or jog or even run,
Its when you fly,
When all seem sly,
Now, the most important are looks,
and you don't give a thought about books,

This time is for fun till your core,
wait there is more,
For these years make you,
the real you,,
Make use of them so you don't have any regret or even fret,
When you look back,
On your memories rack,
And remember your carefree days,
Still carefree....
-always

Love

Love yourself first,
Then someone else…..
- self love

That's me

Beautiful and ugly,
That's me,
Good and nasty,
That's me,
Smart and dumb,
That's me,
Active and numb,
That's me,
Superior and inferior,
That's me,
Deserter and warrior,
Yes, that's me,
Popular and lonely,
That's me,
Chained and free,
That's me,
Infinite love and Infinite hate,
That's me ,
That's me,
That's me.

True Beauty

They say your reflection matters most,
Some say its beauty that's internal,
I say it's none,
True beauty is when you are happy,
And your insides are glowy....
.-mirror is a lie

Shilpi

If only

He was a young boy,
A beautiful one,
Always dejected he was,
There were silent screams in his head
Had tons of friends but none were true,
Walking on the sidewalk,
Tears streaming down,
His heart felt like a million pounds,
His mind was full of thoughts,
Thoughts which were useless had no need,
But still were there,
If only he had someone to talk to,
Then he would still be here.
- vent it out

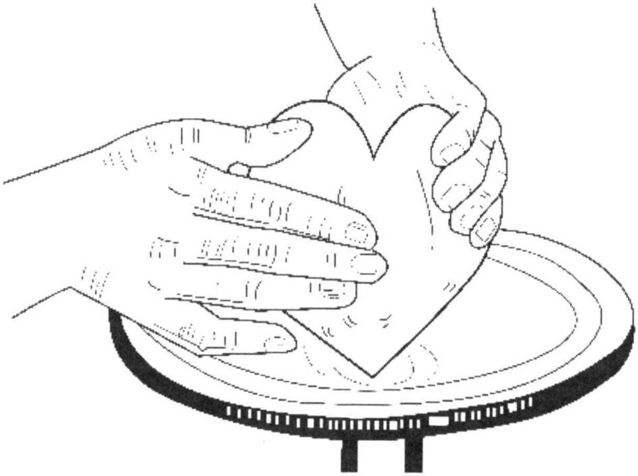

SHILPI

Clay

Don't let your thinking be like clay,
That anyone just anyone can shape it.....
- moist

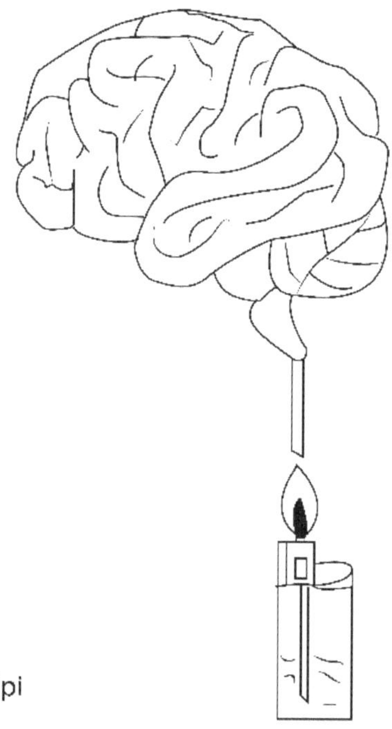

Shilpi

Ignite

The mind is a place of mystery,
It holds magic and secrecy,
From the eye of the mind we are blind,
Not using the powers,
To limits we are bind,
The flame of knowledge have subside,
So ignite,
So ignite,
Powers of The mind I invite,
So ignite.

Smell

"Don't you just love it when you go to an unfamiliar place, and the smell greets you with a wave of nostalgia….."

Shilpi

Pluviophile

I love that earthy whiff,
When it rains,
I take a deep breath ,
And it does wonders.
-to you rain lovers

SHILPI

Scenic Beauty

On a misty day,
I followed a path,
Which led me to the woods..
The air I breathed was so fresh so pure,
I enjoyed from my core,
Trees were all around,
Serenity in everything that was to surround,
That I found pleasure in being in closure,
The foliage was green,
Beauty in everything that was being seen,
Wished that time would stop,
I heard a sound,
A sound soothing to my darkest despair,
I knew it would repair,
That was the sound of rain so mellow,
Falling on ground that was covered in yellow,
Finally with a breath so deep,
I promised secrets to keep,
Bade farewell, to the sweet sweet smell.
-Rain in fall

Shilpi

Stormy

The sky was getting heavy,
All along the levee,
The sky felt gloomy,
All of it truly moved me,
Pitter patter the rain fell,
The air was filled with an earthy smell,
Droplets fell on my chin,
They went right through my skin,
Somewhere I saw a quick flash,
Then I heard something crash,
The sky went from blue to grey,
The cold rain gave me another spray,
The wind began to howl,
Who knows what was waiting to prowl,
I ran as fast as I could,
Searching for something good,
Feet throbbing -heart racing,
This was a fear I was facing,
Finally I saw a warm light,
Ever so bright,
And when I saw a lawn with a red Gnome,
I knew I was home!

SHILPI

A Question to Humanity

I just want to ask ,
Why make weapons?
when the world craves peace,
Why have borders?
When all wish unity,
Why be decisive?
When all want honesty,
With a dash of Harmony,

A border is nothing,
but a line so fine,
Which can make all intoxicated,
Without a drop of wine,
That all are filled with wrath,anger and hatred,
Destroy a bond of Humanity that is so sacred,
Some even sow the fruit of jealousy,
Just for the sake of supremacy,
God! no one wants this complexity filled with such Intensity!
Someone please answer !
Why make weapons?
When the world craves peace,
and wish to live with ease.
-toxic borders

SHILPI

Presence

"Let your presence to someone be like a cold rain
shower on dry- parched land"
-soothing

An Ode to Humanity

Let us all raise our hands,
to pay on Ode to humanity,
Put a cease to this insanity,
As we all stand under wreath,
on this land given to us by Heaven as heath ,
Let us bring her some freshness,
Shower love on her till her core,
So, she brings the life back on shore,
Surrounded we were,
with all kinds of harms,
I pray to god ,
"Receive us in your loving arms'
So, let us pay an ode to humanity,
Put a cease to this Insanity.
-Respect

Sensations

I just love that feeling when you hear a soft whisper,
Feel a loving touch,
Or a light kiss,
When no one is around,
It means you are loved......
by your angels
-angelic

SHILPI

Come, Embrace

Last night full of gratitude,
I felt a change of attitude,
My eyes felt wet,
And warm,
I don't know when tears of love began to form,
Out of love and thanks,
I don't know when,
I extended my arms into the space,
Welcoming all who wanted to embrace,
I felt a presence,
a presence so soft,
That my heart began to defrost,
I wanted,
No… I needed to hug,

That presence in the empty space,
Tears flowed,
And my insides glowed,
I closed my arms and embraced,
I embraced me,
Last night God told me I hugged her,
That she is me,
Residing in my spirit so free.
-God is love

Heaven or Hell with A Touch of Luck

The satisfaction of burning heart,
The never reaching the end of start,
All this heaven and hell,
Lives inside your well,
All them angels,
All them demons,
Are by your side ,
Just choose with whom you want to ride,
What is heaven?
What is hell?
They are nothing but a part of yourself,
Well,
Some wish for lady luck,
to smile upon them,
to you,
No such thing as luck,
Will help you earn a single buck,
All that you need is nothing but hard work.
-Superstitious

SHILPI

Crazy Day !

One day I went through an old alley,
Which was just beside a beautiful valley..
The path adorned with roses on the side,
The attractiveness was amplified,
suddenly,
I caught a glimpse of a thing,
lying all alone,
untouched,
in the middle of the lane upon a stone
The thing was working like a magnet,
and I did the role of metal,
Attracted to it like a bee to a petal,
they were a pair of glasses,
the lens were the colour of Rainbow,
They smelt somewhat like molasses,
They had a unique glow.
I put them on,
Somewhat fascinated,
They changed the world going on!
The sky was raining gold!
flowers blooming,
carpets of meadows began to unroll!
Fairies dancing and Leprechauns singing,
Spell bound I stood,
frozen on the spot,

once senses regained,
when I was no longer chained,
I threw the glasses on the road,
and things were no longer absurd,
I just ran as fast as I could,
not once looking back,
once home ,
I told my mom,
Now you must be thinking,
that my heart would be sinking,
That my mom would not believe a word of this story,
but she listened ,
listened steadily,
each word carefully,
until she caught me off guard and completely pale,
when she unfolded the glory of her own true tale !
-Surprise surprise

Vera

We are going to Vera,
Where they greet us Buonasera,
It's a place so special,
Where the birds chirp all day hum at night,
It's a place where they never Fight ,
Where the waves kiss the shore,
It's a place where you live life more,
The fields stretch on for miles and miles,
This place is full of rosy aisles,
So come with us,
If you must,
To Vera where they greet us buonasera,
The music seems unrealistically holy,
That we dance all night slowly,
The stars shine on our face ,
Take us to a whole new place,
Let me take you to Vera,
Where they greet us buonasera.
-utopia

Pencil

A pencil serves a million things,
From drawing to writing to aid in itching,
A pencil serves a million things,
You use it to give birth to dreams,
to write recipes on "how to make whipped cream?"
It helps you to ace any test,
if you make it your friend that's best,
so use it wise and use it well,
Cause, This is the piece,
On which your dreams dwell.
-lead to make you lead

One Wish

One wish is all that's needed,
to ease all that was once impeded,
To make all in command,
then, one wish is in demand.
I need just one wish,
to stop all this gibberish,
just one wish to make flying fish.
To get that one wish,
all you need is a kiss with destiny,
one a beautiful day that's sunny,
Under clouds that rain honey!
When I get mine,
I'll wish for something ever so fine,
Noooooooo! not gold,
Something even more bold,
Something that'll make me do many dances.
Well, I will wish a million more chances!

Acknowledgements

I would firstly like to thank God and my beloved Angels without them this wouldn't be even possible,

I would also like to thank all those who have been a part of this tremendous opportunity,

I would like to thank my maa and papa, who kept me going on with their infinite love and support,

I thank my brother Virat who didn't understand my poems with his young brain yet, supported me wholeheartedly,

I would like to thank our beautiful world which inspired and motivated me at every little moment.

THANK YOU!

About the Author

Aarna joshi is 15 year old teen who has a unique way of perceiving this world,

She finds beauty in the smallest of things and loves to stare at the falling rain,

She loves to do all things that an average teenager does movies, music, k-dramas, books, and what not!

The only difference is her deep passion for poetry.....

And her thoughts.....

On how to encourage humanity and touch people's hearts with her poetry.